MANAGING
YOUR MONEY

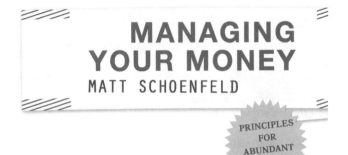

MANAGING YOUR MONEY
MATT SCHOENFELD

PRINCIPLES FOR ABUNDANT LIVING

BEACON HILL PRESS
OF KANSAS CITY

Copyright 2008
by Matt Schoenfeld and Beacon Hill Press of Kansas City

ISBN 978-0-8341-2387-8

Printed in the
United States of America

Cover Design: Arthur Cherry
Internal Design: Sharon Page

Library of Congress Cataloging-in-Publication Data

Schoenfeld, Matt, 1967-
    Managing your money : principles for abundant living / Matt Schoen-
feld.
        p. cm.
    Includes bibliographical references (p.   ).
    ISBN 978-0-8341-2387-8 (pbk.)
    1. Finance, Personal—Religious aspects. I. Title.

    HG179.S2963 2008
    332.024—dc22

                                                            2008034923

10 9 8 7 6 5 4 3 2 1

CONTENTS

FOREWORD

Four years ago I received a phone call from a total stranger who asked me if I would be willing to hear his idea for helping Christians with their personal finances. I felt compelled by God to meet with him. That stranger, Matt Schoenfeld, soon became a good friend and faithful ministry partner.

Matt was helping the homeless, prisoners, low-income folks in the urban core, and rich people in the suburbs learn to be better money managers. His approach was simple, user-friendly, and grace-based. It was flexible, fun, and focused on ministry more than money. I thought it was the best mix of practical money management advice and spiritual insight available.

Matt has combined his practical advice and sharp spiritual insight to offer this book to Christian homes, schools, and financial coaching ministries. *Managing Your Money* will give you confidence to do what may seem impossible: spend less than you make.

You will learn seven secrets to becoming a better manager of what God has given you. As you put these secrets to work and become a better steward of your resources, you will grow spiritually and have a greater impact on the Kingdom.

Managing Your Money will help you as you seek to follow Christ in your finances as well as your faith; the two cannot be separated. Blessings to you as you honor Him.

Steve Weber
Director of Stewardship (retired)
Church of the Nazarene

INTRODUCTION

In the long run, we get no more than we are willing to risk giving.
—Sheldon Kopp

"We just can't seem to make ends meet!" How many times have you heard that? Have you said it yourself? As I travel around the country teaching personal finance seminars and meeting with families to provide one-on-one financial coaching, it's a phrase I hear often.

Recent figures reported by myFico show that nearly 40 percent of consumers have non-mortgage debt totaling more than $10,000 and that 15 percent of credit card holders carry balances of more than $10,000.[1] Many Americans are clearly living beyond their means.

"Matt, we make $97,000 a year, and we can't make ends meet." I often hear complaints like this from people who make even more than that as well as from folks of more modest means who come to the Abundant Living Biblical Financial Fitness workshops I teach.

From those who earn a medium income to those who have a high income, their *perception* is that they can't live within their means and get all their bills paid. If that's how you feel, you have a lot of company. This book can help you.

Everyone is dealing with the rising costs of gasoline, groceries, and a college education—and almost everything else. I lead a nonprofit organization, so I'll be the first to admit that it's definitely a challenge to scrape together a salary that allows me to provide for my two kids, who seem to never stop eating—and they're only seven and five years old! I feel for parents of teenage boys! I can't help but wonder what groceries will cost when my children are teenagers.

What's somewhat curious is that while people seem so strapped, personal incomes have quadrupled since World War II, and inflation has averaged only about three percent a year. So why do so many feel as if there's never enough money?

I think the key word—and I used it earlier regarding making ends meet—is *perception*. While there's no disputing that many key necessities such as food, energy, and transportation cost more, the reality of how we spend our money is often overlooked in articles decrying the economy and contending that the government is responsible for life being so hard for hardworking men and women. Living within our means is both imperative and often elusive.

There are spiritual and practical insights into

how families can make ends meet. I find in my interaction with families that the reality of *where* the money is being spent is a lot more significant than the *cost* of gasoline, groceries, clothing, or other items.

Most of the persons who come to our workshops take a simple, biblical financial check-up test. You can take the test yourself at <www. abundantlivingministry.org> if you like. This tool helps folks score themselves on how well they're managing the money at their disposal.

What routinely happens when people take the financial check-up test is that they're forced to admit that they really don't know where their money is going. Furthermore, many divulge that they're not doing any financial planning. You have company if you fall into this camp as well.

While living within your means is a tough practical and spiritual challenge, the core issue is not the amount of money you make but how you manage what you have.

The goal of this book is to let you in on seven secrets—seven key practices—that my wife, Cynthia, and I have used to win the money management battle. Not only have these habits helped us live within our means and keep our financial ship afloat, but they've also enabled us to save for future needs, give generously to God's work, and start a full-time personal finance training ministry to help others in this critical area of life and discipleship.

For Christians, an important benefit to getting a handle on finances is the ability to give generously to God's work. It's not about getting rich or being showered with blessings. There's certainly nothing wrong with having money or being blessed financially, of course, unless money becomes the gauge for judging success.

The gauge of true biblical financial success is not wealth—it's faithfully managing what God is providing for you so that you can serve the Lord in the fullness of your personal calling. My hope is that the seven secrets that have helped me will help you as well so that as you find financial peace, you'll also find peace spiritually. Peace in Christ takes you beyond the financial component of money management into the spiritual realm that will produce the fruit of the Holy Spirit in all areas of your life.

ONE

THE SECRET
OF SELF-CONTROL

Self-respect is the fruit of discipline; the sense of dignity grows with the ability to say no to oneself.
—Abraham Heschel

With the average salary of a player in the National Football League at $1.4 million per year, the strategy is pretty clear on how to make ends meet these days—just become a professional athlete!

Do you know how much a left-handed relief pitcher winning only half of his games makes? It's depressing. I'll just say that I've already started teaching my five-year-old son, Will, to throw left-handed. With the current rate of inflation and the state of the economy, this is clearly his best bet for a secure financial future. "Come on, Will—throw another strike in here! No, Will—left-handed! Left-handed!"

Ladies, not to worry—we have you covered too. Perhaps you've heard of the popular female Indy racecar driver Danica Patrick. With race income of almost $1.2 million in 2007, which doesn't include endorsements or speaking fees, and more than $3 million so far in her career, we're talking about pretty impressive earning power. And she's won just one race at this writing.[1]

It's pretty simple: to make ends meet each month, you should become a pro athlete. Movie star or recording artist are both good career choices too. Implement this simple strategy, and you don't even need to read the rest of this book. Now that's money management made easy!

Of course, you probably see the flaw in this money management strategy. The odds of attaining such lofty levels of athletic prowess or Hollywood fame are about nine gazillion to one. The odds are even worse for winning the Publishers Clearing House sweepstakes.

Day-to-day money management is tough for all of us, and living within our means seems to be the grand-poobah challenge. For followers of Jesus, putting our faith in lotteries or other long shots is *not* the path to follow. Yet, how are we to make ends meet with the cost of milk and gasoline and practically everything else going through the roof?

I coach many families on personal finances as part of my Abundant Living Personal Finance Training Ministry. I know firsthand how hard it is for those who are just trying to slog through the financial trenches of life—especially single moms, folks in economically depressed parts of the country, and those who may not have had the opportunity to pursue higher education. My hope is that this book will give you a few insights into things you can do to win the battle of living within your means. It will give you information that is key to winning the personal financial management war.

I was joking about the strategy of becoming a pro athlete, but I do think there's something to be learned from athletes such as Priest Holmes, Lance Armstrong, Brett Favre, Michael Jordan, and others like them. What do these incredible athletes have in common? Week after week, month after month, year after year, despite setbacks, injuries, and in many cases personal tragedies, they continued to play their sport at the highest level.

Priest Holmes was not drafted by a team in the National Football League (NFL) after college, but he became the greatest running back in the history of the Kansas City Chiefs. Lance Armstrong overcame cancer and won an unprecedented seven consecutive Tour de France bicycle races. Michael Jordan was cut from his high school basketball team but went on to become what many consider the greatest basketball player ever. Brett Favre beat an addiction to drugs and went on to help win the Super Bowl and an unprecedented three consecutive Most Valuable Player awards in the NFL.

What traits do these athletes possess that enabled them to compete at a consistently high level year after year? What gave them the drive and internal motivation to keep trying despite the many setbacks they faced? And what can we learn from them that will help us be better at managing the resources God has provided for us?

Two words define them: *perseverance* and *self-discipline.*

A good friend of mine from college, Jeff Myers, told me not long after graduation that he wanted to be as good at public speaking as Michael Jordan was at playing basketball. That statement left an indelible mark on me. I asked myself, *What am I so passionate about that I would invest the time and effort necessary to allow me to function at a high level for a long time like Holmes, Favre, Armstrong, or Jordan?* The persistence to keep trying and the self-discipline necessary to practice and improve are the very traits you and I need to master money management. The question then becomes: *Can I transfer the qualities of persistence and self-discipline to my personal finances?*

Brett Favre started 275 consecutive regular season and playoff games as the quarterback of the Green Bay Packers.[2] It's an iron-man streak that's second to none. Favre showed up day after day to do his job and play at the highest level.

You and I must develop that same kind of stick-to-it attitude when it comes to our commitment to live within our means. No matter what, just as Favre did, we must show up, get the job done, and with the steely resolve of a Hall of Fame quarterback staring down the defense, stay within our means. No excuses, no trying to justify. The alternative of bulging debt levels, relational stress, and spiritual powerlessness is far too costly.

Proverbs 30:7-9 encourages us to live within our means by directing us to the path of moderation: "Two things I ask of you, O LORD; do not refuse me before I die: Keep falsehood and lies far from me; give me neither poverty nor riches, but give me only my daily bread. Otherwise, I may have too much and disown you and say, 'Who is the LORD?' Or I may become poor and steal, and so dishonor the name of my God." It's not how much we have—it's how we manage the daily bread God provides that matters most.

By following the wisdom of this proverb, you'll avoid either striving for riches or succumbing to a poverty mentality, and you'll be able to live on what God is providing for you *right now*. I minister to people of all economic levels across the country, but I've worked with only a couple of families in 13 years that I felt truly did not earn enough money.

If you want to get bare-bones honest about managing your money, take into account the parable of the talents found in Matthew 25:14-30. Jesus indicates that God is doling out more funds to those who are doing the best job of managing the money. Psalm 24:1 tells us that everything belongs to God anyway, so He can do with it as He sees fit.

What the parable of the wise money managers teaches us is that if we feel we don't have enough money right now, the answer is to do a better job of managing what we do have. It's often easier to throw up our hands in despair and lament that we don't have enough than it is to take a hard look at spending habits and determine whether the problem is actually that we're not managing well what we already have.

If you haven't been managing well what the Lord has given you, humble yourself before Him and ask for forgiveness. Then commit to better stewardship of what you have.

No rocket science is involved in living within your means. You must spend less than you make each month. It's necessary to come up with a strategy to ensure that your income outpaces your expenses. This approach assures that you have money to add to your savings each month and that you have money to give generously.

The reality is that not many people, Christians included, are following this common-sense approach. Remember the folks I mentioned in my personal financial coaching ministry? Their average debt, excluding the mortgage, was just over $50,000. That's more than $50,000 owed on credit cards, vehicle loans, school loans, and other debt. In most cases, these folks had very high incomes well above the national household median, which is currently around $47,000. However, they still struggled to live on what they were bringing home each month. Self-control was not on their radar screens.

Just as self-control is key to the success of pro athletes, self-control is key when it comes to finances. The secret to financial peace in Christ—perhaps the granddaddy of all financial secrets—is simple, profound, and elusive: the Holy Spirit must be invited into your finances so He can give you the self-control to flourish with the gifts He has given you.

We live in a consumer-driven, materialistic culture that makes it difficult to spend less than we make. Nearly 70 percent of those who use credit cards do not pay off their balances each month. I mentioned earlier that average Americans have a good chunk of debt that they have difficulty paying off aside from their mortgage payments.

The reason for that, generally speaking, is a

lack of self-control—one of the character traits produced by the fruit of the Spirit. My intention is not to make you feel guilty. Motivation by guilt won't produce lasting results. What is needed is a personal revolution produced by Holy Spirit-inspired self-control

In Galations 5:22 Paul lists the fruit of the spirit: love, joy, peace, patience, kindness, goodness, faithfulness, gentleness, and self-control. Self-control may be the forgotten fruit. Other traits in Paul's list are more popular and celebrated—love, joy, peace, and patience. Self-control is easy to overlook.

Yet self-control seems to me to be the key to achieving just about every good thing in life and faith. When we use self-control in our habits, relationships, and practices, it's a manifestation of God's very nature and essence coming forth in our lives.

Perseverance, self-discipline, and self-control are not highly praised in our culture today. The Lord must break into our hearts and heads for us to recognize the benefits of following the path of self-control. Just as Lance Armstrong showed perseverance and self-discipline, he reaped the benefit of his rigorous training and practice. It paid off by nearly a decade of Tour de France wins. Your results are not likely to be so widely known and may not seem so dramatic. However, the consequences of living within your means will be no less revolutionary to your spiritual as well as your financial life.

God's Word reveals a truth that enables us to develop the power of self-control so that we can live within our means. It will turn what Satan would have us see as a restriction into what the Lord wants us see as a new field of blessing.

Brett Favre was not an overnight success in the NFL, and Lance Armstrong had to beat cancer before he could wear the yellow jersey. The Greek translation of *self-control* is *egkrateia*. It indicates one who can master his or her passions and connotes a process of training. Just as an athlete must train to become adept at his or her sport, you and I must train to develop self-control.

Repetition is one of the keys to making practice effective. When I played basketball, my teammates and I shot 30 free throws at the end of practice every night. Not once did we take a night off. That repetition led to game success.

My daughter, Mattie, is a budding ballerina. Even though she has a natural affinity toward ballet, it's in practicing the same core elements over and over that her art is perfected.

Renowned Packers football coach Vince Lombardi was known to run the same play in practice 40 or 50 times until the players got the timing and assignments down perfectly. The repetition led to five world championships in seven years. Many players who were coached by Lombardi later in life testified that while the winning and championships were great, the discipline and lessons they learned *through the process* were their greatest reward. It was learning self-control that led to their later successes in life after sports. Training ourselves to live with self-control leads us to faithfulness in managing God's money and deepens our confidence in walking through life with Him.

I've followed the Abundant Living money management system to manage my own finances for more than a decade. The repetition built into our financial system through years of practicing self-control is the very thing that makes it simpler to stay on track. Did Favre get tired of throwing touchdowns just because he threw more than any other quarterback to ever play the game? No way! And I don't tire of following a money management system that works to keep us living within our means, giving generously, and planning for the future. The key to finding success is being willing to practice and employ self-control.

Are there financial fumbles and times we've had to punt along the way? Certainly, but the consistent practice of employing self-control makes the process more straightforward and easier to follow the more you practice it.

So like Jordan, Favre, Holmes, and Armstrong, it's time to practice and persevere. Skip dessert once a week to practice some self-control. Get a salad instead of fries. Go for a walk when you'd rather watch television. Do more research for a better deal when you really think you've found the right item at the right price. Wait.

At first, shoot for small successes. Then let them add up and become bigger successes. Before you know it, self-control, and the Holy Spirit, will flow through your life and your finances in a new way. You can do it with God's help!

By the power of the Holy Spirit, you can develop self-control and train yourself to live within your means. Self-control will be important as you move to secret number two for managing your money.

TWO

THE SECRET OF PAYING NO INTEREST

By constant self-discipline and self-control you can develop greatness of character.
—Grenville Kleiser

Our society has converted from a culture of savers to a culture of spenders—unfortunately relying on debt to secure that which we must have right now. The second secret of good money management that allows us to live within our means is to pay no interest.

Employing the Holy Spirit fruit of self-control, you must be committed to paying no interest on consumer purchases. Don't go into debt on any purchases other than a home mortgage, a business start-up, or school loans. If you already have unsecured debt, there are small steps you can take to bring you to a new way of doing things. In recent years, I've become more and more impressed that this is one of the most vital of all financial strategies.

If you're thinking, *Oh, great! I'm sunk because I already have consumer debt,* don't despair. Let's have a quick chat about good, better, and best.

I'm not writing from the ivory tower; I understand the real world. I know you must have transportation to get to work and must buy new tires and purchase food and perhaps pay off debts at the same time. If you've been using credit cards and not paying them off each month, I recommend you start at the "good" level and stop using the cards completely. Use carbon-copy checks when you make purchases. Start saying no to paying interest on anything that depreciates in value, such as vehicles, computers, and consumable items, such as food, clothes, vacations, and entertainment.

At an alarming rate, people are ignoring the fact that the power of compound interest that works for you when you save money also works against you when you go into debt. Simply put, the amount you owe grows. Because average credit card interest rates outpace long-term stock market rates of return—approximately 15.4 percent to 10.5 percent respectively—avoiding negative compounding may very well be a more important strategy, at least initially, than taking advantage of positive compounding in investing. At a recent seminar I taught in California, during our debt reduction plan exercise a young couple was alarmed to learn that the interest rate on their credit card was 31 percent. Prior to attending the seminar, they had no idea their rate was so high. The compounding effect of interest in their case was devastating. Heeding my advice, the couple called the credit card company and received a reduction in their interest rate to 8 percent. Just like that, their interest rate dropped 23 percent. They will save thousands of dollars as they pay off their upper four-figure balance.

If possible, get the momentum moving in your direction so you can move from good to better to best. Right after Cynthia and I were married, we had to take a loan to buy a car. For some reason we had driven separately somewhere, and I was following her in her more-than-used Mazda, which had also been recently pummeled by hail and was covered in dents. As I drove along behind her, I noticed a large gray patch on her back tire but couldn't tell what it was. When we got home, I saw there was a large chunk of tread missing. She was not safe driving to work and college. Based on the number of miles on the car, the hail damage, and the cost of the repairs needed, it was time to get a new car. We sold the faithful Mazda for $400 in a garage sale and put that money toward a down payment on a new car.

Using the proceeds of the old car and dipping into our savings, we made a good down payment and took a three-year loan for the balance. After doing our research, we chose the least expensive make and model available at the time. Would it have been good to pay cash? Sure! But that wasn't reality. Here's how we moved from good to better. We paid off the three-year loan in one and a half years. Getting a safe, reliable car for my wife was good. Paying it off in half the time was better. The best is that we drove the car for 15 years, saving up so that we've been able to pay cash for the other new and used cars we've bought during our 16 years of marriage. We've never again paid a nickel of interest on a car.

We've also bought furniture, first for our apartment and later for our house, and we paid for Cynthia's college education. She waited a year to get in and worked as a special education teacher, earning the money to cover all her tuition and book costs for three years. We paid off our credit card bill every month without fail. The bottom line: we've never paid interest for furniture, school loans, or credit cards, and only a small amount of interest on one car.

We did this in the mid-90s when we were earning a combined gross income of $22,000 to $39,000 a year and living in the Midwest, so we were not flush with cash. I worked for an investment company, and Cynthia cleaned houses and worked at the school to save money to go back to college for a degree in occupational therapy. We lived simply, faithfully gave 10 percent or more to the Lord, and saved everything we could. Granted, it helped a lot to have a wife who liked saving money as much as I did.

How did we do it? We refused to pay interest, lived within our means, and took small, steady steps. The reality was that we had to trust the Lord and dig a little deeper to avoid paying interest.

Is God asking you to dig a little deeper when it comes to your personal money management habits? Cynthia certainly dug deep to go back to college to earn a second degree after the first one did not pan out. I've worked with countless families who have dug deep to pay off their debts and make a workable spending plan. You definitely have to dig deep to refuse to pay interest on things like cars, credit cards, and furniture. But you can do it. Start today, and commit to stop paying new dollars on interest.

If the time is coming for a new vehicle, and you don't have the funds saved up to buy it with cash, either drive your car a bit longer and keep saving, or wait until automobile makers offer a zero-percent interest deal. Zero-percent interest has become fairly common in recent years. By making the payments every month, in three to five years you will have paid cash for the vehicle with no interest dollars out of your pocket. There are the same zero interest deals available for furniture and other items.

Pray about these kinds of purchases before you make them. My point is to show that there are ways to get what you need and want without paying interest if you employ some patience and know-how. If you use the same-as-cash option and make regular payments, you'll get what you need. Best of all, you will have paid cash for it without plunking down a large additional amount for interest.

Beware of these options if you don't think you'll have the discipline to make the monthly payments. If you fail to pay off your purchase in the allotted time, you'll get socked with the retro interest and maybe some fees to boot. But this can be a winning strategy for you, as it has been for me, to purchase large-ticket items. There have even been times when we had the cash on hand, but because we were confident we could make the payments on time, we got the dual benefit of the new item while keeping our cash invested in a mutual fund.

On other occasions, we've saved up the amount needed and paid cash. Flash cash around, and you'll often get a nice discount.

You may be wondering if it's really that big a deal. How much money are those interest payments costing anyway? Let me tell you: it can be a bundle.

Look at these examples and see what the bottom-line savings would be if you employ the early-payment, same-as-cash, or buy-it-for-cash strategies. First, here's the biggest opportunity to save: a home mortgage.

If you took out a conventional, 30-year, fixed-rate loan of $150,000 to purchase a house, your monthly payment would be $899 a month, using an assumed interest rate of six percent. If you faithfully make your payment every month for 30 years, you will pay a total of $323,757 to own the home, not including the down payment, taxes, insurance, or closing costs. That's $150,000 for principal and $173,757 in interest payments.

Now let's chop that interest amount down to size a bit. If you can come up with just 50 extra dollars a month to pay toward the principal loan amount, your total interest payments drop to $147,084. You will save $26,673. Pay an extra $100 a month, and the savings jump to $45,586.

Want to save the really big bucks? If your cash flow situation will allow you to take out a 15-year conventional loan with a 5.5-percent interest rate instead of a 30-year note, your monthly payment will increase to $1,225, $326 more per month than the 30-year loan. However, you will be out of debt in half the time, and you will reduce dollars spent on interest by a whopping $103,144.

Using this example, the total spent on interest drops from $173,757 to only $70,613. Could you use that extra $100,00 over the next 15 years?

It may be a stretch to come up with an extra $326 a month for the mortgage payment, but even if you took out the 30-year note so that you are not locked into the higher payment, the extra principal payments of $50 to $300 a month will save you significant money over time. This is your best opportunity to save a substantial amount of money by saying no to paying interest.

Let's look at how much you can save by not financing the purchase of a new vehicle. If you purchase a 2008 Honda Accord and finance $22,386 at 4.99 percent over four years, your monthly payment will be $515.43.[1]

If you make all 48 payments on our sample Honda, you will pay a total of $24,740.64 for your new wheels. If you had paid cash, you would have saved $2,354.64. Aren't there a lot of other ways you could use that money over the next four years? Maybe a mission trip, your daughter's braces, or a romantic anniversary cruise. I'm sure you have a wish list of things you could do with it. That's why we paid cash for the new car we bought. Believe me—if I can do it, just about anyone can do it.

Let's explore one final example of avoiding interest. You see newspaper ads every holiday if not every weekend—huge cost-slashing deals on sectionals, sofas, headboards, and dressers; the furniture sale to end all sales. But it's only this weekend. You must act now! Your head tells you there will be another sale next holiday or next weekend, but your heart says you can't wait that long.

Just for fun, let's say new furniture, if not a fundamental need, is a pretty serious want. So you're off to the furniture store to save yourself big bucks.

Even on sale, the items you want carry a $4,500 price tag. Because the money is not exactly on hand at the moment, you finance the purchase for three years at 6.99 percent. Your low monthly payment comes to only $107.74 for 48 months.[2] Sweet! The car will be paid off the same month as the furniture! The total amount of interest you'll pay for the new sleeper sofa and all its friends now stands at $671.52.

But there's another way to get the new furniture and keep the six hundred dollars and change in your wallet. It will take some discipline, but you can still get your furniture today and pay no interest.

Cynthia and I have used this strategy a number of times, allowing us to furnish our home and never pay one penny of interest: shop for your furniture when the stores offer zero-percent interest deals.

Remember: the finance manager is banking on your not making the payments on time so that they can sock you with all the interest and other finance charges and late fees. But you can be the winner if you make the monthly payment on time every month. Set it up as an automatic withdrawal from your bank account to ensure that you don't forget to send a payment.

Total dollars in your pocket:

Purchase	Amount You Saved in Interest
House	$103,144.00
Car	2,354.64
Furniture	671.52
Total Saved	**$106,170.00**

As you can see, paying no interest results in serious savings. Any of these examples results in enough money saved to make a positive difference in living within your means. Because every dollar you spend on interest is essentially a dollar down the drain, learning to say no and beat creditors at their own game will mean a lot more dollars in your pocket over time. That will translate to a lot more money available to give back to the Lord, save for future needs, or spend on other important stuff. Employing the "Say no" strategy will also go a long way in helping you be successful with the next secret in being a good money manager.

THREE

THE SECRET OF RESPONSIBLE AUTOMOBILE OWNERSHIP

Drive-in banks were established so most of the cars [on the road] today could see their real owners.
—E. Joseph Cossman

Did you know that if you really want to, you can buy a luxury sedan that costs more than $100,000? Lexus, Beemer, Mercedes Benz. Take your pick. Any one of these high-end automobile manufacturers will be glad to offer you one of their leather-seated, gold-plated, platinum glove-boxed smooth rides. We paid $71,500 for our first house in 1994. To think—I could have purchased a really nice car instead.

There's certainly nothing wrong with these cars, but don't lose track of what the real cost may be. I know a guy who has frequently lamented to me that his retirement savings will not be enough. Bring up the topic of retirement, and there's visible panic on his face. However, this same individual has bought more than 20 vehicles during the last 25 years. It's good to have a hobby, but in this case it turned out to be a tad expensive.

In his defense, I will say that a couple of those cars went to his teenage kids, but still, buying a car almost every year takes its toll. If he had driven just six cars and put the money he saved into an average stock mutual fund, by a conservative estimate he could have a minimum of an additional $500,000 in his nest egg. I've never had the heart to tell him that he's driving his retirement.

Secret number three to managing your money is pretty basic and can save you thousands of dollars over your lifetime: drive the same vehicle for at least 10 years. Sounds easy, right? Okay—now really do it. Here's an idea to help you: don't watch television. Every five minutes there is a commercial to convince you that your vehicle is no longer good enough, cool enough, or trendy enough.

I'm not suggesting that you must buy a used car either. If you stick to the plan and drive your car for 10, 12, 15 years or more, I'm not against buying new and then driving it until it drops. To be honest, my wife and I have not had great luck with used cars. But if you buy a reliable model, you can save even more of your hard-earned dollars by getting a good used car and then driving it for 10 years or more. According to *Consumer Reports*, the three most reliable carmakers are Honda, Subaru, and Toyota.[1] General Motors and Ford have made some improvements in recent years as well.

Sure, cars depreciate in value 15 to 20 percent a year on average, but that's an average. If you buy a new model that holds its value and drive it for a long time, the peace of mind and warranty of a new car may suit your family better. Plus, it won't hurt your pocketbook in the long run. This boils down to personal preference. The linchpin here is to drive the car a long time.

Consumer Reports reveals that if you keep your vehicle for 15 years, or 225,000 miles of driving, you will save nearly $31,000 compared to buying the same model every five years. Playing the trade-in game costs real dollars when you factor in depreciation, taxes, fees, and insurance. And if you invest the money you save, you'll gain an additional $10,300 in interest income during that time, assuming your savings earns five percent a year.[2]

Our Honda Civic served us well for more than 15 years. It got terrific mileage, and other than routine maintenance, it cost us next to nothing. In an effort to help someone else who needed reliable wheels, we recently sold the car to a single mom for less than half its value. It was still worth $1,300 after fifteen years, and we paid only $11,500 for it in 1992! That great little car is still going and saving money for another family that needed a good deal on a car.

The secret of automobile ownership alone

may be enough to get the budget balanced. And we've not even touched on the amount of savings you will enjoy if you buy more fuel-efficient cars. Those savings will single-handedly put Junior through college—or at least buy his books.

Want to super-size your savings? Not only will you save thousands by driving your car for a decade or more—you also get double and triple savings bonuses through the additional money saved on lower car insurance and lower property taxes for older cars in states that collect personal property taxes. While the amount saved will vary depending on make, model, and your particular insurance coverage, as a general rule, driving the car longer will probably save you $300-$500 a year per car on taxes and insurance. If you own two cars and save $1,000 a year—that's money you can put in your emergency fund or vacation fund. You can save more by increasing your deductibles to $1,000 or $2,000, and put even more cash back in your pocket. You must make sure the extra cash is on hand in the event you have an accident or claim, but saving that money will be easy if you're following the wisdom in secret number three.

You may be wondering, *Well, this is all fine and dandy, but does anyone really drive a car for more than 200,000 miles?* Fair question. Even if it's still running, won't it start to look pretty ratty?

Here are some tips to help you extend your enjoyment of your car for as long as you drive it. I'm convinced that the main reason people start yearning for a new car is because it looks dirty or worn. Normal scratches and dings are going to happen, but if you can avoid serious damage and perform the routine maintenance, it's amazing how good an older car can look. Here are some simple strategies to help you enjoy your current wheels and save thousands of dollars for 12 or 15 years or more:

Clean it frequently, inside and out. This helps prevent premature rust, extends the life of the carpet by removing dirt and sand, and keeps you feeling good about your older car. When your car begins to look its age, detail it more frequently.

You can wash and vacuum the car yourself at a self-serve carwash to save money and save even more if you wash and vacuum it at home. Cynthia keeps a Swiffer cloth in the glove box so when she's waiting to pick up the kids at school, she can give the dash a quick once-over. There are lots of little habits you can develop to keep your car looking nice.

Follow the recommended maintenance schedule in the owner's manual. Yes, this will cost you some money, but it's money well spent. The little bit spent on maintenance is significantly less than the big ticket hit that comes from not doing the routine stuff. We have money pulled electronically from our checking account each month into a separate mutual fund money market account for auto maintenance and insurance. This guarantees the money is there for scheduled maintenance. We never take the car to the dealer for maintenance unless the item in question is under warranty. You can save big dollars by finding auto shops that specialize in your make of car. It has been our experience that by forming a relationship with the repair shop, we've built trust, saved money, and helped a small business owner in the process. Repair costs have been on average 30 to 50 percent less that going to the dealer.

Use only the fluids that are recommended for your car. When it comes to motor oil, transmission oil, and so on, don't risk gumming up the engine with something that's 12 cents cheaper per quart.

Buy a set of inexpensive rubber floor mats and install them during the winter months, especially if you live in a region that gets frequent snow. Get the kind with high edges to collect all the salt and slush. These mats protect your carpet and the regular floor mats, extending their life. They're also easy to wash. Clip them up at the self-serve carwash bay and blast away with the power-wash gun.

Limit snacks to items that can be vacuumed up. Accidents happen, especially if you have kids. Give them snacks that are easy to vacuum up and won't get ground into the carpet. You can also get travel cups with lids so that beverages go into their mouths and not onto the upholstery.

You can save thousands of dollars by driving your cars until they drop. If you do a little work to keep them maintained, you'll have more money to spend on life's needs and wants that you deem to be more important than a car. After all, in the end a car serves only to get you from point A to point B.

FOUR

THE SECRET OF GENEROSITY

*The habit of giving only enhances the
desire to give.*
—Walt Whitman

This secret I'm about to share seems counterin-
tuitive, I know. I'm suggesting that giving money
away will help you manage your money so that
you can live within your means. *Huh? How could
that work? I'm barely paying the bills as it is.* Conventional wisdom says that if you give more
away, you'll have less.

Everyone seems strapped these days, struggling to just get by, and turning to experts for advice. What I find troubling is that many financial
planners dissuade people from giving generously.

An article in *Real Simple* magazine gave the
typical "reduce your giving" advice. In an experi-
ment engineered by the magazine, professionals
in the field were employed to help four women
improve their financial plans. The women maintained spending diaries for a month, and then a
planner analyzed their actual expenditures and
gave recommendations on better ways to meet
their long-term goals. The premise of the exer-

cise is an excellent one; however, some of the advice disturbed me.[1]

One of the young ladies in the study, who was tithing to her church, was encouraged to quit giving so much: "If Lyndsey wants to have the down payment [on a house] sooner, she might have to reconsider tithing 10 percent of her income until she reaches that goal, since the rest of her spending is so lean." Aside from a redundancy issue—use of the term "tithing 10 percent,"— the only other real advice the planner gave was to spend more money on fun. Give less, spend more. Typical.

While I agree that Lyndsey's spending for the month was frugal, and overall she was doing a pretty good job with her finances, the financial planner evidently had no qualms with 22 percent of Lindsey's income going to a car payment and other transportation costs or 12 percent of her income going to entertainment. It's not that I have a problem with those percentages for her expense categories. My point is that there are usually other areas where we can trim back, but those areas were evidently off limits while *giving* was on the chopping block. It's my firm opinion that Lindsey received bad advice, both financially and spiritually.

Interestingly, Lyndsey, who is in her early 20s, was earning by far the least and giving by far the most of the four women profiled. The other women, who were seven to twenty years older than Lindsey, earned 79 percent, 83 percent, and 172 percent more than Lyndsey respectively while giving only 0.007 percent, 0.009 percent, and 0.002 percent of their monthly incomes to charity compared to Lyndsey's commendable 10 percent. Not one of the other three gave one percent away, and not one financial planner suggested that the three women increase their giving. Dollar for dollar, Lyndsey gave $230 a month to her church while the other three gave a combined grand total of $69 to charity. Aside from her car, Lindsey was debt free, while the other three were still digging out.

Lyndsey gets it. At a very young age, she understands the joy of giving, and the worst thing she could do for her financial plan would be to give less. The secret to true biblical financial success lies in giving generously. In fact, if you want to really improve your finances, you should not give less—you should probably give more!

Giving should be the foundation of all Bible-based financial planning. Giving doesn't guarantee that everything else will fall into place, although it often does. Giving makes it more likely that you will fall on your face before the Lord, and that leads to deeper fellowship with the Giver of all good things.

Paul writes,

> Remember this: Whoever sows sparingly will also reap sparingly, and whoever sows generously will also reap generously. Each man should give what he has decided in his heart to give, not reluctantly or under compulsion, for God loves a cheerful giver *(2 Cor. 9:6-7)*.

A joyful motive coupled with a generous heart creates a powerful one-two punch of generous living. When you start with giving, it enables you to take the Lord's financial seeds and plant them in a mission field that will generate a harvest that will transform your life and the lives of others. When giving is your top priority, spending rarely gets out of line with your income or your heart motives. Giving becomes your spiritual turbocharger.

Generous giving will help you mature spiritually and help you develop a heart that seeks God's heart—a heart that burns with passion to give all resources back to Jesus. Above all else, God is a giving God. As you grow in the grace of giving, you become more like Him.

Paul says in 2 Corinthians 9:10: "He who supplies seed to the sower and bread for food will also supply and increase your store of seed and will enlarge the harvest of your righteousness." Not only does this reiterate that all we have belongs to God in the first place, but it also shows that by sowing generously with our resources we'll enlarge our harvest of righteousness. Paul does not say that if we give more we'll get more money—he says we'll get more God.

According to the *New American Standard New Testament Greek Lexicon*, in the broadest sense *righteousness* means the state of one who is as he or she ought to be; the condition of one's heart that is acceptable to God. It's the doctrine concerning the way in which a person may attain a state approved of God, such as integrity, virtue, purity of life, rightness, or correctness of thinking, feeling, and acting.[2]

Don't miss the deep meaning of this passage: If we give generously, we will be as we ought to be, and we will better reflect the Giver, who gives lavishly and continually.

The harvest—the fruit of our relationship with God—will increase as we generously give. The fruit of our righteousness in relationship with God will expand as we give back to Him of our resources. The net result of this righteous harvest, as promised in verse 10, will be that God will provide more seed for us to sow into His kingdom. The fruit of God's labor will be to give more resources to His faithful stewards so that they can sow more for His purposes.

"Did not our heart burn within us?" (Luke 24:32, NKJV), the disciples asked. Christlike giving to the disciples on the road to Emmaus brought new passion and spiritual enlightenment to their hearts. Further, giving will increase the spiritual power in your heart: "I pray that out of his glorious riches he may strengthen you with power through his Spirit in your inner being, so that Christ may dwell in your hearts through faith" (Ephesians 3:16-17). His very nature is to give glorious riches. As we, too, learn to give glorious riches, we'll be strengthened in our inner being, setting up an abode in our hearts where Jesus can dwell and exhibit His power. Give, and His power will be given to you, pressed down, shaken together and running over. (See Luke 6:38.) The passage in Luke goes on to say, "For with the measure you use, it will be measured to you." Here Jesus uses a similar analogy to Paul's teaching on sowing and reaping. These examples of abundant giving lay the foundation of New Testament generous giving.

Giving leads to greater connection to God and experience of His love. "I pray that you, being rooted and established in love, may have power, together with all the saints, to grasp how wide and long and high and deep is the love of Christ, and to know this love that surpasses knowledge—that you may be filled to the measure of all the fullness of God" (Ephesians 3:17-19). The result of giving is that it will root us in His love.

Like a fencepost set in concrete, giving cements us in His love. It gives us clearer insight and knowledge of the love we all desperately crave, a love that will fill us up.

God is always giving. Malachi 3:10 states that He'll pour out so much blessing we won't have room to hold it all when we bring the fullness of our giving to Him without holding back. For in addition to the unparalleled offering of His Son on the Cross for our sins and the endowment of the Holy Spirit's indwelling work to regenerate us and seal our resurrection, God is continually giving to us spiritual gifts, knowledge, breath, blessings, insight, provision, wisdom, and the life that is truly life.

And as Malachi alludes, He's not doling it out with an eyedropper either. Matthew Henry's commentary states, "We should give liberally, with an open hand, and cheerfully, with an open countenance, being glad we have ability and an opportunity to be charitable."[3] The secret that many miss in Jesus' words "It is more blessed to give than to receive" (Acts 20:35) is that you get *more* when you give, not less. If you sow generously, you will reap generously. Henry concludes, "Works of charity are so far from impoverishing us that they are the proper means truly to enrich us, or make us truly rich."[4]

Deceived by the twister of truth, many in the

Church have tried to tell us that the results of faithful tithing or generous giving will be champagne, jewels, and German cars. This line of thinking takes the ultimate blessing and distorts it down to the lowest common spiritual denominator: health, wealth, success, and physical possessions. The mystery and miracle of lavish, generous giving is that until you find that "truly rich" actually means attaining the image of the giving God, giving with the slightest hint of an ulterior motive to receive in return will produce only a desecrated facsimile of the Father.

When our definition of "truly rich" means we're enveloped in His intimacy—the ultimate blessing of basal connection to His very giving essence and nature—we'll finally know what generous giving truly is. Giving of this high quality won't produce a Beemer; rather, it will produce the satisfaction and transformation of being how you should truly be.

The passage in 2 Corinthians 9 goes on to say in verse 11, "You will be made rich in every way so that you can be generous on every occasion, and through us your generosity will result in thanksgiving to God." There's that word again: rich. But it does not say you'll become rich so that you can have creature comforts and more of them. It says you'll be made rich, if you really understand true riches, so that you can give more on every occasion.

I find it very interesting that the phrase "harvest of righteousness" occurs only two other times in the New Testament. In Hebrews 12:11 the author states, "No discipline seems pleasant at the time, but painful. Later on, however, it produces a harvest of righteousness and peace for those who have been trained by it." Another passage, James 3:18, relates a similar theme: "Peacemakers who sow in peace raise a harvest of righteousness." The common thread of seeking a harvest of right living will be increased peace for you and those around you. Thus, giving abundantly, exercising discipline—a key component to living within your means—and being an agent of reconciliation will foster the elusive peace that passes all understanding. And you thought we were just going to balance the budget!

Hopefully you've become convinced of the spiritual power of giving, but how will it help you in a practical way to not spend more than you make? First, giving generously will help you strike a balance in life so that you'll joyfully give to God first, enabling you to better prioritize the use of that which is left over to meet the needs and wants of you and your family.

Since I was 19 years old, the first check of each month has been back to the Lord. In 22 years I've yet to have a month when I did not have enough. Believe me—there were some lean months because of job losses, sick kids, wrecked cars, and humble salaries. You've probably experienced those kinds of months too. But somehow, giving first tends to make you a better manager of the amount that's left over. When you give last, something will always spring up and steal the dollars you intended to give to the Lord. "Without faith it is impossible to please God" (Hebrews 11:6). Give in faith, hope in God, and He'll lead you into a life of love.

When you give to Him first, you're saying, *I trust you, Lord, to take care of me and get me through this month.* It's not magic; giving first or tithing does not mean that you're locking God into doing your bidding. However, that law of sowing and reaping with a cheerful heart and right motive is like gravity. You can't escape its effect. Giving first in faith will produce the harvest of righteousness—the intimacy with God we most dearly need.

THE SECRET OF PLANNED SPENDING

Some couples go over their budgets very carefully every month. Others just go over them.
—Sally Poplin

Nothing is intolerable that is necessary.
—Jeremy Taylor

Sarah was so overwhelmed by paying her bills and dealing with her finances that she had given up. She quit opening her mail because it caused too much stress. Unfortunately, piling the bills in a corner and trying to forget them is a strategy that leads to more trouble. The false sense of relief won't last long.

Finances are one of those distressing things in life that we all face on a monthly—if not daily—basis. Unless you're blessed with the resources to hire a personal assistant who will take care of paying your bills and managing your money, you can't escape financial maintenance.

Eventually, Sarah got fed up with her fear of finances and her looming, unopened mail. She came to me for financial coaching, and we went to work setting up the key structure her finances lacked: a spending plan and a system to implement it.

Because I'm often seen only as the practical money guy—the "Minister of Money," as my friend Darren tabbed me—what many folks don't know about me is that I make unbelievable omelets. It's my hidden skill. However, my skill was completely lost on my daughter, Mattie. She's not an egg enthusiast.

Not too long ago on a Saturday morning, while we were letting Mom sleep in, I enthusiastically asked my kids, "Who wants an omelet?" Will, my egg-loving number-one son, erupted "I do. I do. I do!" Mattie, on the other hand, gave her typical you-know-I-don't-like-eggs glower.

Not to be dissuaded in sharing my gift, I repackaged the question: "Okay, then. If you don't want an omelet, Mattie, would you like some cheesy eggs?" She brightened up and exclaimed, "I do. I do. I do. I love cheesy eggs!"

It's often all in the way we look at it, isn't it? Cheesy eggs are just an omelet with a kid-friendly name. However, to Mattie, repackaging made all the difference. Maybe you need to repackage your approach to money management or your cash flow system to find a better and more appealing way to do it. When it comes to regular money management, it may be a matter of doing away with the negative-sounding budget and welcoming the cheesy eggs of financial management: the spending plan. Even calling it a "cash flow system" sounds intimidating.

However, a *spending plan* doesn't sound too bad, does it? Hey—it has the word *spend* in it, right?

I have bad news for Bud Selig, the commissioner of Major League Baseball. Baseball is no longer the national pastime—it's been replaced by shopping. What was the first thing we were told to not give up following 9-11? Shopping, of course!

Retail therapy is a cure-all. "Take two credit cards and call me in the morning." The reality is that you're going to spend money, so let's not pretend that a budget will put an end to it. Men don't shop as often as women do, but when they do, they tend to buy high-dollar toys. The reality is that men and women are going to spend money.

The Bible doesn't caution us to save every penny and not spend money. But *loving* money—now that's a different thing. The Bible repeatedly warns us to flee the *love* of money.

Spending allows us to enjoy some of the good things in life that money can buy. It allows us to take our kids to the circus and share in their excitement when the elephants walk two feet in front of them. Adhering to a spending plan brings the freedom and the power of financial management that allow us to win the battle of the pocketbook. We'll also attain the joy and freedom that comes from serving the Lord well as we do a good job of managing what He has given us.

A good spending plan and a good system for managing money are the two things that most of the people who come to me for advice don't have.

I meet thousands of people every year through the financial workshops I teach. When those folks take the biblical financial checkup offered during the workshop, which is available at <www.abundantlivingministry.org>, the two areas in which they usually score the lowest are long-range planning and following a spending plan. Many of them are not aware that having a spending plan is fundamentally different than having a budget.

A workable spending plan is a two-part process. Even ardent budget enthusiasts usually have only a one-part plan, and that part is often incomplete. This is why I'm anti-budget and pro-spending plan.

You may be saying to yourself, *He's just trying to trick me into following a budget. What's the big difference between a budget and a spending plan?*

One big difference is that a budget is not a

useful financial tool unless you also track your expenses to determine where your money is really going; a budget is just a lot of numbers projecting what *might* happen with your income and expenses. That's not reality.

To become successful at managing your money, you need a system to track your monthly spending. You'll find a monthly expense tracking sheet in Appendix 1 at the end of this book.

Expense tracking allows you to compare actual money earned and spent to your original projection. It's the tracking of these expenses that's the key to effectively managing your money. It's less painful than you think.

A budget is an "orderly method for living beyond your means." A budget becomes, as it is typically used, a financial straightjacket.

"Honey, here's the new budget we're going to follow. So don't spend more than $32 on food this month, and don't spend money on anything else." That rarely goes over well.

Rather than a budget, use a simple system to allow you to effectively manage the money you're entrusted with each month—a spending plan.

Let me define a spending plan: *A flexible money management tool that helps one allocate resources, live within his or her means, plan for the future, track spending, and meet obligations.* The plan consists of two parts.

The Spending Plan, Part 1

The first part of the spending plan is a projection of income and expenses—what many would call a traditional budget. In the projection stage of your plan, you'll write down how much you expect to have coming in after taxes during the next month. You'll also write down an estimate of what you expect to spend, divided into several categories. You'll do this every month.

These two things will get you off to a good start; unfortunately, this is where many people stop. The problem is that the plan is only a rather vague idea of how much money you will spend and where it might be going. It's an estimate rather than reality. You still don't know *exactly* where your money is going. It's a helpful exercise and an important part of the process, but it's not a financial *plan*.

What's missing—and it's missing in most people's plans—is what I call the *feedback loop*. Are you spending $300 or $500 a month on food? That's a big difference. Is transportation costing you $700 a month, or is it closer to $900? Where *exactly* is your money going?

The Spending Plan, Part 2

The second part of a fully functioning spending plan includes maintaining some type of money management system that enables you to know exactly where your money is going each month.

This part of the spending plan helps you make important financial transactions on time and shift spending to different needs as they arise, and it provides a framework to make good decisions about how you spend your money.

Without the two-part spending plan to help manage your money, it's sort of like giving an engineer all the raw materials to build a yacht but not providing a plan or a blueprint. The result could be a dinghy, a cruise ship, or something that won't even float!

After working in the investing industry for seven years, and teaching personal finance for more than a decade, I've found the only way to keep the financial ship afloat is to utilize the two-part spending plan.

Using a spending plan is a biblical concept. Not surprisingly, the biblical model drives us right back to the idea that we're to do the loving thing with our resources. The wisdom literature writer shows us a unique live-within-your-means command that ranks right up there with other powerful biblical decrees such as praying continually, loving God, and forgiving those who trespass against you.

In Proverbs 27:23-24 we're instructed, "Be sure you know the condition of your flocks, give careful attention to your herds; for riches do not endure forever, and a crown is not secure for all generations." Because a sheep or goat won't fit in your wallet, the 21st-century application of this verse is to give careful attention to your money. The implication is powerful: if you don't pay careful attention to your resources, they'll disappear; riches do not endure forever. It's important that we keep track of how our money is spent.

Failure to develop and follow a spending plan increases the likelihood that you'll lack key financial information, end up wasting money, and struggle to gain financial freedom. Money that you don't pay attention to will tend to disappear. That's not good!

If you fail to stay on top of your finances, you could wind up hurting others besides yourself, such as your family. Remember: "A crown is not secure for all generations."

Without a spending plan system to help you pay careful attention to your flocks and herds, you could hurt your kids, your grandkids, and even your great-grandkids. The implication of this verse is that you may affect the entire course of your family's future by utilizing the simple financial tool of a spending plan.

Balance your checkbook today—it may bless your grandkids someday. Track your expenses each month—you may be able to make a sizable gift to ministry when you're old and gray—or maybe well before then. Spoiling your grandkids may seem a long way off, but it's never too soon to think about putting yourself in the position to be a blessing to the Lord and others.

I obviously was not thinking about my grand-children when I was in college. I was having a hard enough time just trying to get a date. How-ever, the most significant money lesson I ever learned happened during those four formative years, and it was a perfect illustration of the need for a spending plan.

At the start of each semester, my parents gave me a check for the amount they determined was enough to cover my room, board, tuition, and books. They made it clear that if I ran out of money, I was on my own. Spending money for other incidentals was up to me. During my last two years, I had to pay a portion of the tuition as well.

I didn't realize it then, but this was the best lesson in following a spending plan I could have received. Thanks, Mom and Dad! I took my par-ents at their word and never tested them to see what would happen if I ran out of money.

Talk about paying careful attention! I worked two jobs to make sure I had spending money. I watched every dollar and projected my expenses for the whole semester regularly to make sure I would make it. During summer breaks I worked to earn and save more for the next year. I set up two checking accounts to keep the money separate: fun money in one account and expense money in the other. Not an elaborate plan, but it taught me the nuts and bolts of living within my means. I was proud to contribute to my tuition from money I earned. These were important lessons in working hard and managing money.

Implementing a spending plan is the most crucial step in getting your financial house in order and maximizing your ability to live within your means. The list below shows you the benefits of setting up and following a monthly spending plan.

The Benefits of a Spending Plan

A spending plan provides several benefits:

- It tells you where your money goes each month, which allows you to make good financial decisions.
- It helps you spend money wisely and avoid wasting it.
- Once it's fully operational, you'll enjoy freedom and confidence in your money dealings as never before.
- Your plan will be a positive tool to help you keep check on your values and priorities so you do the loving thing with your resources, as opposed to dealing with a budget that often makes people feel they're constantly failing.

- Your future planning will happen automatically, because you'll build planning into your system.

Now that doesn't sound so bad, does it? Interestingly, the Barna Research Group has found that while 25 percent of us say we follow a budget, in reality only 10 percent of us actually stick to the plan of how we will spend our money.[1] That's why so many people struggle with personal finances. If the research is right, 90 percent of us cannot say with certainty where our money is going.

One of the biggest advantages of our spending plan for my wife and me was that it actually helped us spend *more* money. This is a good thing—just ask my wife. Early in our marriage I was being too tight with our money and was having a hard time letting go of it. Being miserly or hoarding money is just as bad as overspending or abusing credit cards. My drive to control our money blocked our ability to enjoy some of the simple things in life that are also blessings from above. (See James 1:17.) After talking it over, Cynthia and I agreed to set up "mad money" accounts for both of us as part of our monthly entertainment funds. Having a reasonable amount of fun money each month was probably the best financial move—and marital move—we've ever made. It gave us the freedom to spend our money, and it actually helped us enjoy life more. Whether I added a CD to my music collection, saved money for a special golf trip, bought a toy for one of the kids, or took a friend to lunch, having this mad money gave each of us the freedom to spend within the confines of our overall plan and helped me manage money better and in a healthier manner.

The apostle Paul was a fan of spending plans. In 1 Corinthians 16:2, Paul sounds like the national spokesman for the Middle Eastern Association for Spending Plans when he says, "On the first day of every week, each one of you should set aside a sum of money in keeping with his income, saving it up, so that when I come no collections will have to be made." Remember: this is a guy who saw Jesus after the Resurrection, the foremost evangelist of the Early Church, the writer of the majority of the New Testament, and the key leader of early Christianity. Paul tells us that every week we should give according to our income (live within our means), not spend all we have but save money up (plan), and set aside sums of money for specific purposes (use a spending plan). Following Paul's advice will set you on course to live within your means.

As with any other new habit, tracking your spending requires rolling up your sleeves and working at it for about a month. However, once it becomes routine, you'll be surprised at how simple and effective it is to oversee your monthly financial planning.

Horace, a noted philosopher, once said, "He has half the deed done who has made a beginning." So if you're willing to track where you're spending your money, the time you invest to work at this task will create an opportunity for you to gain newfound freedom and control of your personal finances.

Check out the five-step process listed below to assist you in your spending plan.

Setting Up Your Personalized Spending Plan

Step 1: Determine your income—your take-home pay.

Step 2: Set up spending categories.

Step 3: Plan what you'll spend in each category.

Step 4: Track your expenses.

Step 5: Review and modify. Compare your actual spending to targeted amounts, and adjust your spending as needed.

Appendix 2 of this book is a blank spending plan to use to gather and record the information you need to build your personal plan. There's also an example of a completed spending plan for reference purposes. It will provide you with some suggested spending categories that you can change or modify to fit your life. The point is for this to be flexible.

After you've recorded your monthly income on the spending plan and subtracted the amount you pay in taxes, you'll arrive at a key figure in your plan, your net spendable income—your take-home pay. If other items are taken out of your earnings before taxes, such as retirement savings or tax savings plan contributions, make sure these expense amounts are accounted for in your savings or personal household categories or the appropriate category.

Once you've determined your net spendable income, make your best-guess estimate of the amount you think you'll spend in each of the expense categories you've listed. When you've allocated a target expense amount to each category, add those figures to determine your total monthly expenses. One key thing to note: the amounts in the categories may change from month to month. This is to be expected, and it allows for flexibility. I find it's very rare when any two months are the same. So each month, take a couple minutes to plan out what you think you'll need to spend in each category. At the end of each month I map out what I think the next month's income and expenses will be. This allows us to plan for what to expect in the upcoming month.

As you start to track where your money is going you may find your projected targets are way off. That's fine. The point is not to be perfect; the point is to use the tool to help you live within your means. Don't give up if it does not go exactly as planned the first month—or second or third months. Remember: almost no months go exactly as planned. Rather than becoming frustrated, use your new knowledge to help you set more accurate targets for the following month.

If your income varies each month—-a challenge I, too, have faced—you can still make the spending plan work for you. You will need to gather some information on what your income has been for the last six to twelve months to allow you to base your plan on a conservative income estimate. Don't pick your best month, and you probably should not pick your worst month either. The key for those with fluctuating income is not so much trying to figure out what the income will be each month. Rather, it's setting aside a sizeable amount on a good month and saving it to carry you through a lean month. Again, this requires some God-inspired planning and self-control.

After you've examined your pay stubs and checkbook to help determine your income and expense amounts, subtract your total projected expenses from your net spendable income, or take-home pay. This will give you a ballpark esti-mate of where you are in terms of your monthly spending plan. The goal is to try to have a sur-plus each month, or at least to break even. Re-member: you'll probably need to make some modifications, so don't worry if it looks as if you're spending more than you're making at this point. You can correct this problem once you start tracking your expenses, which will enable you to figure out what's really going on with your spending and ensure that you're living within your means.

Answer this question honestly: *Am I serious about tracking where my money goes each month?* The two best ways to do this are by using either the Abundant Living Personal Finance Organiz-er, which is available at <www.abundantliving-ministry.org>, or by using a financial software program like Quicken or Microsoft Money. What's significantly more important than the for-mat is the commitment to actually do it. More than any other strategies mentioned in this book, tracking your expenses will enable you to live within your means. However, tracking is proba-bly the hardest strategy to implement.

Use either a written method or a computer software method for tracking your spending. Each has its own advantages. The main point is to find the system that works for you and then use it and stick with it. After a couple months of tracking, you'll begin to hone in on an average amount you tend to spend in each category. Choose the more conservative estimate as your target for both your income and your expenses, especially if your income fluctuates. As you get better at tracking, you'll find it becomes easier to save money. You'll also get a better feeling for the value of money. You may be less willing to easily part with it when you've invested some time in trying to be a better manager.

Your spending plan will serve you well as a flexible money management tool. It's an integral component of making your system work. Don't be discouraged if you spend more than your targeted amount in one or more categories each month. That's not a huge deal. But if it happens consistently, modify your plan so that it's more in line with your actual spending patterns. Just don't spend more than your net spendable income (NSI). Hopefully, your plan will help you spend even less than your NSI. If you see you're likely to exceed the $500 allocated in the personal expense category for childcare costs for a month, by tracking and comparing actual expenses to your target you'll be able to cut back in another area so that you can still stay within your means.

The key is to make sure you know what your

net spendable income—or a close approxima-
tion—will be for the month and adjust your
spending patterns accordingly. By tracking your
spending progress, you'll have the information
you need to make the necessary modifications.
Again, you're *planning* how to spend rather than
feeling as if you can't spend or are somehow
cheating on your budget. Sticking to the princi-
ple of living within your means will give you confidence and will give you the freedom to spend
funds in areas where you have wants or needs.

The benefits of paying careful attention to
your "flocks and herds" are numerous: you'll be
able to give generously, live within your means,
plan for future needs, beat materialism, and
bless God, self, and family. Utilizing a spending
plan on a monthly basis will boost you into an
elite category of money managers. Remember: in
the parable of the talents, God rewards the good
managers, so you'll likely have the opportunity to
share more love, have greater freedom to minister, and possess the means to pass on more of
Christ's blessing by implementing this key financial strategy.

THE SECRET OF PAYING BILLS IN YOUR SLEEP

Good ideas are not adopted automatically. They must be driven into practice with courageous patience.
—Hyman Rickover

If a boy has no money to handle, how will he learn to handle money?
—Jan Karon, from *Home to Holly Springs*

Is paying bills one of the highlights of your week or month? I know—it's boring. But we all have to take care of this mundane but important aspect of life. What if you found a way to get it all done but spend less time and energy on it?

Last week I paid all my bills, and I didn't do a thing, didn't lift a finger. No, I don't have a personal assistant, and I didn't talk my wife into doing it. I'm the designated bill-payer in our family. I paid all the bills automatically.

One of the keys for helping our family with money management over the years has been to arrange to have the amount due on as many bills as possible deducted automatically from our checking account or billed automatically to our credit card. Do not charge your bill payments to your credit card, though, unless you pay the balance off every month and use a spending plan to track your spending. We rarely use checks except to pay the credit card bill, for our giving, and for bills that occur only once or twice a year such as life insurance premiums, homeowners and car insurance, real estate taxes, and so on.

All our other monthly bills—15 to 20 in all—are paid automatically. Those include payments for mortgage, gas, electricity, telephone, and water; missions giving; cable television and the monthly movie services we sometimes use; Internet service; health insurance premium; monthly savings for car repairs, vacation, real estate taxes and insurance; tuition for the full-day kindergarten program; and cell phone service.

I don't have to do anything to get all those bills paid on time every time. I simply record the payments on our tracking sheet when it's convenient for me, and it eliminates having to keep track of due dates. I prefer using automatic withdrawals or direct billing rather than paying bills online for one simple reason: these options require less work for me. Online bill paying would still require time to log in and pay the bills. If your cash flow is tight, you may need the flexibility of paying online, but if you can get your system down, automatic payment is simpler and will save you time in the long run.

As great as it is to streamline all or most of your financial transactions, the biggest benefit of automating your bill paying is that you'll always feel as if you're ahead of the bill-paying game. And that greatly increases your chances of living within your means and avoiding the stress of money management.

Here's how I made automatic bill paying work for me. Initially, I contacted all of the places I wrote checks to each month and asked if they had an auto-pay or direct billing program. The form needed to sign up for automatic payment is often right on the monthly bill you receive. Once that application was sent in with the check paying the bill, all future bills were deducted automatically. Each vendor either sends a one-time confirmation letter of the day the payment will be withdrawn, or they send a monthly bill that confirms the day the amount will be deducted from your account.

At the beginning of every month I take out my expense tracking sheet from my personal finance organizer (see chapter 5 for information regarding setting up a spending plan), and I enter every automatic bill payment from my account during the month. I record all the payments the first day of the month and subtract the amounts due from my checking account even though many of the bills will be paid from my account later in the month. The exceptions are payments that are automatically charged to our credit card. In this case, I still track the expense into a spending category on my tracking sheet; however, no money is deducted from my checking account. The cash will change hands when I actually pay off my credit card bill each month. I feel as if I'm always ahead in my bill paying. It also helps me know how much money will be left for other expenses that may fluctuate month to month.

The most significant factor is that all the bills are paid, and I don't have to write the checks, drop them in the mail, or buy stamps. I also don't have to think about any major bills again until the next month. That relieves a lot of stress.

Cash Flow Concerns

I am paid once a month, so I know on the first day of the month exactly how much money we're going to have coming in, and that number is not going to change.

If you can swing it, another strategy that works well to control cash flow, regardless of how many times a month you get paid, is to get to the point that the money you earn in January is the money you will live on in February. That allows you to feel as if you're ahead of the game rather than playing catch-up. If this strategy is not possible for you at the present, keep it in mind for the future.

When I was paid twice a month and my wife was paid every two weeks, we followed the same process of entering all the bills ahead of time. Some planning is necessary to be sure that your automatic payments are not set up for the seventh of each month when your check is going to be deposited the 15th. You can usually choose the dates you want payments automatically deducted, so pick dates to match your pay cycle.

Monthly Financial Management Steps

Once you get your system in place, you can complete all the tracking of your expenses and basic financial planning in two or three hours a month, allowing yourself time to give careful attention to the resources God has entrusted to you.

Following is a summary of the things I do each month to complete the money management plan for our family and the approximate amount of time it takes to complete each task.

Step 1. I project take-home income for the coming month. Based on that amount, I plan how much I intend to spend in each of the categories I've set up. (10 minutes)

Step 2. I record the deposit of my check on the expense tracking sheet or check register and add it to the checking account balance. (1 minute)

Step 3. I write checks for all expenditures that have not been set up on auto-pay plans. I record these transactions on the expense tracking sheet. The more bills you pay by check, the more time this step takes. (5 minutes)

Step 4. I record auto-pay bills or bills charged automatically to my credit card on the expense tracking sheet and deduct the amounts from the checking account balance. (10 minutes)

Step 5. I track non-reoccurring expenses made by check, debit card, or credit card, such as food, gas, gifts, or miscellaneous purchases or services. (30 to 45 minutes)

Step 6. I file receipts needed for tax purposes. (5 minutes)

Step 7. I compare the amount spent to my target amounts each week, then adjust spending as needed based on our needs. (20 minutes)

Step 8. I compare my monthly income or projected income to the total month-to-date expenses to ensure we're living within our means. I adjust spending as necessary. (10 minutes)

Step 9. I reconcile the checking account each month. (20 minutes)

Step 10. I enjoy my free time!

One final strategy I suggest that you use to automate your monthly financial planning is to learn the power behind the secret of prepaying. For the most part, your long-term financial planning can happen automatically. Employing this tactic will take a greater amount of self-control and planning than anything we've discussed yet; however, once in place, the secret of prepaying will guarantee you live within your means today and every year God gives you breath. Prepay today, and you'll enjoy peace of mind tomorrow.

The secret of prepaying could be described as advanced living within your means. As you implement what you've learned, you can get to the point of setting up your monthly spending plan in such a way that you actually begin to prepay for future expenses while still paying your current expenses. Remember: good, better, and best. Work toward this goal as you're able.

Each month you'll set up automatic payments that move funds from your checking account into a separate savings account for future expenses such as your emergency fund, your next vehicle, vehicle maintenance expenses, vacations, children's education, retirement, and other periodic expenses such as car insurance or life insurance. If your employer offers a retirement plan, you're already employing part of this strategy as you prepay your retirement living expenses by contributing to the plan. However, by living below your lifestyle level, you can also begin to prepay the above-listed expenses so that you're prepared for the future. I have a set amount pulled from my pay each month and placed in a 403(b) account (a retirement plan for nonprofit organizations) and into a money market account at a mutual fund. The money market houses our emergency fund, vacation fund, car fund, and tax and insurance fund. Again, because these funds are transferred every month automatically, all our future planning happens automatically as well.

This important strategy will enable you to live out Proverbs 21:20—"In the house of the wise are stores of choice food and oil, but a foolish man devours all he has." When the emergency comes, when the next vehicle must be bought, or when you need to pay for your child to go to college, you'll have financial peace that passes understanding because you won't have to worry about how to pay for these important future expenses. The money will be waiting in your savings accounts. Because you've elected not to use up all you have but instead live below your means, you'll be in a unique position to tap your stores to bless others.

If you can practice the self-control of a professional athlete, incorporate the wisdom of God's Word, set up a monthly automated prepayment plan, and wrap it all up in a disciplined yet flexible spending plan, you will have mastered the most difficult aspects of money management:

long-range planning and having a month-to-month financial plan. After doing your part to the best of your ability, you can ultimately rely on the Lord for your daily bread.

THE SECRET OF
A HAPPY CHEAPSKATE

That man is the richest whose pleasures are the cheapest.
—Henry David Thoreau

I confess that I'm a cheapskate. The reason I haven't brought it up sooner is because, after all, you're already reading a book on living within your means. You're probably thinking, *Isn't that enough?*

I don't really get why so many people don't see frugality as an important part of money management. Why in the world would people not want to get good deals, fight to keep their money in their own pockets, and stretch their dollars as far as they can possibly go? Do they think that it would be too much work? Maybe.

Maybe if we repackage the cheapskate persona into a more positive image, people will respond—kind of like my daughter was willing to eat cheesy eggs but not an omelet. Considering that the actual definition of a cheapskate is a miserly or stingy person, especially "one who tries to avoid paying a fair share of costs or expenses,"[1] I don't think I want to wear that label.

Instead of being cheapskates, what if we were shrewd? "Shrewd" means intelligent, streetwise, judicious, and astute.[2] I like the sound of that. Becoming shrewd with your money is the final secret to living within your means. I'm not suggesting a life of unbalanced deprivation or that you hoard all your money, refuse to do anything fun, never give any money away, and never spend money in a reasonable way. Hyper-frugality can be a sign you're still trying to be in control of your money rather than letting God use you to manage His money.

To be successful at living within your means and living at the lifestyle level God is calling you to, it's important to adopt a mind-set of Christ-inspired financial shrewdness. Sometimes this means buying the higher-priced product—yes, the more expensive one. By doing some sharp-witted research, you'll often find that the more expensive product lasts longer and is of higher quality. Therefore, you save money in the long run. Being shrewd requires taking the time to do the research.

Are you willing to do what it takes to live within your means? If it was a breeze to do, there wouldn't be so many people struggling with credit card debt and just trying to keep up.

My observation from coaching families on finances is that that they give in to the feverish pace of life and make *expedient* financial decisions rather than *shrewd* ones. Maybe they're running late, so they grab fast food for the fourth time in a week, or they buy gas for 15 cents more per gallon because it's handy. Maybe they become victims of impulse purchases. None of these things is necessarily bad or wrong; but when you total all the little incidental expenditures, you see a snowball effect. Before you know it, you're living beyond your means.

If you're struggling to live within your means, you must identify the real issue. You can do that by seeking the mind of Christ.

The spiritual man makes judgments about all things, but he himself is not subject to any man's judgment: "For who has known the mind of the Lord that he may instruct him?" But we have the mind of Christ (*1 Corinthians 2:15-16*).

Paul says that a person indwelled by the Holy Spirit must make judgments on all things, including finances. Jesus continually talked about money and financial issues. He taught the parable of the talents in Matthew 25:14-30, He taught to plan and count the cost in Luke 14:28-30, and He taught to give in Acts 20:35, to name a few instances. These teachings will help you live within your means. If you manage your money wisely, plan for the future, and give it away generously, you'll have the mind of Christ and will be a shrewd money manager.

The real issue is not whether you shop at discount stores and buy only used vehicles. The key is to examine your heart and life to see if you're doing your best to manage well what God has given you.

You could be the deal-finder of the century, but if your motive for seeking good deals is fear of running low on money because you don't trust God with your finances, you still won't have peace, even if you're living within your means. Choose to faithfully follow Jesus' teaching in your finances.

So how does a spiritual money mind-set translate to our day-to-day lives and help us balance our spending plan? Here are five ways to build a healthy mentality for finding good deals that will save you money.

"Is That Your Best Price?"

The harmless question "Is that your best price?" should become your favorite phrase when you shop. This non-offensive phrase could save you hundreds, maybe thousands, of dollars each year. You don't have to play hardball or leave the store in a dramatic display of shopping self-righteousness. All you have to do is ask the salesperson in a calm and straightforward manner, "Is that your best price?" Often the answer will be "You know what? I bet we can do something." According to a *Consumer Reports* study, shoppers who ask for the best price get better deals on big-ticket items such as medical bills, appliances, electronics, and furniture 90 percent of the time.[3] It often works on smaller purchases too—household items, clothes, and lawn and garden goods.

Don't go overboard and try this with the checker at the grocery store or Wal-Mart, obviously. "Is that your best price on grapes?" "Is that your best price on milk?" "What's your best price on toilet paper?" But I have negotiated good prices on everything from a nice chef's knife to lamps and other household items. If they say they can't do any better, you're no worse off. Plus, you can say you want to wait on the purchase, check another store, check online retailers, or find another option. My wife and I find that patience puts a buyer in a better position on more significant purchases. It allows you to clarify whether you really need the item or items, gives you more time to research alternatives, and provides you more leverage for getting a better deal.

With certain bigger purchases, you must be willing to walk away and lose the item for the sake of getting a better price. This especially comes into play on houses and cars. Remember: houses and cars are *always* on the market. Just walk away or make an offer of what you're willing to pay. If they reject your offer, you've lost nothing! Sellers hope you'll be afraid you'll never find another house or car or blender that will suit you as well as this one, but I guarantee you that you will.

Remember: "Is that your best price?"

Dare to Compare

If you like charts, you'll love this one. Even if you hate charts, you'll agree it's a good idea. When you comparison shop, keep track of your options. I always create a chart for quick reference to keep me organized. But there's a second step to comparison shopping that takes this strategy to the next level. Not only do I research to compare prices, but I then take my findings to the retailers to play them off one another. This is capitalism at its best.

When we bought a car last year, I had three dealers in three states vying for my business. Remember: in most instances you're in the position of power. Retailers want to sell you something. I was very kind and up-front, but I told the salespersons, "Look—I have this offer from another dealer." When they presented a counter-offer, I said I would think about it. I did this all by phone and e-mail to save my time and money by not driving to the dealerships or playing games with the sales managers. I paid less than invoice price for our new car and saved more than 20-percent off the list price.

When we needed some appliances a few years ago, I had two stores each claiming they would meet or beat any competitor's prices. And they did. I went back and forth a couple times, and we saved over $2,000. When one of the stores dropped out of the bidding, I knew I had hit the bottom.

Little Equals Big

The "little equals big" strategy is sort of the opposite of what we just looked at, saving big dollars on big purchases. In this case, I want to save little dollars on a bunch of purchases. Often, if you save just a little bit, you might be tempted to feel that in the grand scheme of things it's not a big deal. What my family agreed to do is add up all the savings from various items and put the savings into the vacation fund. Thirty bucks here, fifteen bucks there—it adds up more quickly than you think. Knowing that the savings was going to help fund a ski trip in the mountains of Colorado was all the incentive we needed. Cynthia started cutting my hair and our daughter's hair at an annual savings of $210. Setting up automatic payments on our bills saved us the cost of stamps, envelopes, and checks for an annual savings of $110. Dropping cable TV saved us $540. There's $860 right there. "Little equals big" takes on powerful proportions when you have a clear goal for the funds you save.

Coupon Cash

This is not the normal "you should cut coupons" pitch you've heard before. We actually don't use coupons all that much anymore except for those used in our new coupon strategy. There are certain products we know we'll use on a regular basis. Cynthia has started calling the 800 number on the product packaging of products we really like or use frequently, and she asks them to send us their coupons. They do it every time. It takes only a couple of minutes. Now, instead of having to buy the Sunday newspaper and wading through reams of coupons for products we almost never want, we have the coupons of products we know we'll use mailed right to our mailbox. Cynthia has estimated that this strategy saves us $200 to $300 a year.

More for More

Nearly everyone wants to pay less for more, and in a lot of arenas this is a good way to cut costs. However, we've found that paying more for certain products up front often leads to saving more down the road. High-end products are often high-end for a reason: they're of better quality. Buying the cheaper product does not always pan out, even when you do your homework. We did diligent research on minivans and went against our better judgment to buy a make and model other than the one we had previously owned and been very happy with. Our research findings indicated the alternative brand had equal reliability and cost $12,000 less. Unfortunately, the reliability information was not that reliable.

While we did save a lot by getting the vehicle for below invoice, it hasn't been worth it in light of the engine almost falling out of the van, numerous rattles and hiccups, pitiful gas mileage, and automatic door locks that lock at inconvenient and random times without being touched. We've made six trips to the dealer, and the locks have never been fixed. After the last time, they told us they would not try again. Lovely customer service.

I'm no mechanic, but I'm pretty sure that when an engine almost falls out, it is a bad thing. The dealer told me that even though the van was still covered by the bumper-to-bumper warranty, tightening the bolts that hold the engine in place was not covered by the service contract. At my insistence, however, they did finally fix it for free.

This was a life lesson that showed us that even though we saved a lot, we probably would have been better off paying more for a car with a proven track record—even if it meant buying a used car. This is a dramatic example price-wise, but we've had similar experiences with furniture, clothes, and other small-ticket items too. Don't be afraid to pay a bit more for higher-quality products that will probably last longer. It's good stewardship.

LIVING IN THE BLACK

When you live within your means, you are in a better position to be used by God.
—Matt Schoenfeld

If you employ even a few of the secrets you have learned in this book, you will take steps toward living within your means, simplifying your financial life, and attaining biblical financial fitness. It's important that you try to keep things as simple as possible. John Gaule said, "A complex system that works is invariably found to have evolved from a simple system that works."[1]

I want to emphasize that a simple spending plan system will be your greatest ally in winning the battle of living within your means. The spending plan is the tool that can lead you there with God's help.

I am not insinuating that God won't or can't use you if you're not living within your means. That's His department. However, having worked in full-time Christian service for more than a decade, I've seen many talented and gifted servants—lay people, pastors, and church staff members—whose ministries have been hampered or extinguished because money issues and living in the red took a sad, excruciating toll.

There is spiritual significance in living in the black. Spending less money than you make each month over a long period of time will enable you to live out the wisdom found in God's Word and will put you in a better position to serve Him in the unique manner in which He calls you.

I hope you're encouraged and motivated to live within your means as you enjoy abundant life in Him.

NOTES

Introduction

1. John Rosevear, "Getting a Grip on Debt," July 31, 2007, <http://www.fool.com/personal-finance/credit/2007/07/31/getting-a-grip-on-debt.aspx>.

Chapter 1

1. <www.indycar.com>.
2. <www.packers.com>.

Chapter 2

1. <www.edmunds.com/new//2008/accord/100939053/calculator.html>.
2. <www.fnblifetime.com/loancalculator.html>.

Chapter 3

1. Associated Press story quoting *Consumer Reports*, Feb. 28, 2007.
2. "Drive Your Car to Death, Save $31,000," *Real Simple*, March 2007.

Chapter 4

1. "Your Biggest Money Worries, Solved," *Real Simple*, March 2007.
2. <www.bible1.crosswalk.com/Lexicons/Greek/>.
3. <www.bible1.crosswalk.com/Commentaries/MatthewHenryComplete>.
4. Ibid.

Chapter 5

1. <www.barna.org>.

Chapter 7

1. <www.merriam-webster.com>.
2. <www.thesaurus.reference.com>.
3. "Consumer News," *Kansas City Star*, December 2, 2007.

Chapter 8

1. <www.quotationspage.com>.

APPENDIX 1

Expense-tracking Sample

Abundant Living Expense Tracking Sheet

www.abundantlivingministry.org
877-434-9878

Date	Check No.	Transaction Description	T	Amount of check	Amount of Deposit	Balance	Giving	House	Food	Clothes	Ins/Med	Auto	House-hold	Enter-tainment	Savings	Prof. Exp.	Debts
							380	1200	300	75	350	425	150	225	175	325	200
						1500.26											
1	500	Church		225		1275.26	225										
1	501	Mortgage Co.		900		375.26		900									
2	Dep.	Paycheck			1500	1875.26											
2	502	Grocery Store		125		1750.26			125								
2	ATM	Cash		50		1700.26			12			10	3	25			
3	503	Phone Company		27		1673.26		27									
4	504	Dept. Store		78		1595.26				78							
4	505	Car Payment		300		1295.26						300					
5	506	Discount Store		65		1230.26							65				
5	Elec.	Bank		100		1130.26									100		
5	Elec.	Mutual Fund		75		1055.26									75		
5	507	Gas Co.		55		1000.26		55									
6	508	Movies		15		985.26								15			
10	Elec.	Child Relief Ministry		28		957.26	28										
11	509	Gas Station		20		937.26						20					
12	510	Car Insurance		75		862.26						75					
12	511	Discount Store		25		837.26							25				
13	512	Life Insurance		45		792.26					45						
13	513	Child Care		200		592.26										200	
13	514	Credit Card Bill		150		442.26											150
14	515	Grocery Store		95		347.26			95								
17	Dep.	Paycheck			1500	1847.26											
17	Dep.	Paycheck			825	2672.26											

92

Date	#	Description	Amount	Balance	1	2	3	4	5	6	7	8	9	10	11
17	516	Church	127	2545.26	127										
18	ATM	Cash	100	2445.26									100		
18	517	Electric Co.	60	2385.26			60								
18	518	Internet Service	20	2365.26			20								
18	519	Water Co.	25	2340.26			25								
19	520	Grocery Store	75	2265.26		75									
20	521	School Loan	50	2215.26											50
21	522	Gas Station	18	2197.26						18					
22	523	Babysitter	15	2182.26								15			
22	524	Restaurant	30	2152.26								30			
22	525	Discount Store	45	2107.26							45				
25	Elec.	Health Insurance	300	1807.26					300						
25	526	Medicine	5	1802.26					5						
26	527	Plumber	55	1747.26				55							
27	528	Bookstore	17	1730.26								17			
28	Elec.	Bank Service Charge	3	1727.26							3				
29	529	Credit Card-Xtra Pay	75	1652.26										75	
30	530	Child Care	125	1527.26										125	
		Totals		1527.26	380	1142	307	78	350	423	141	202	175	325	275
		Over/Under Target			0	58	-7	-3	0	2	9	23	0	0	-75
		Target Amount			380	1200	300	75	350	425	150	225	175	325	200

APPENDIX 2

Spending Plan Form and Spending Plan Sample

Spending Plan Sample
Monthly Income & Expenses

Monthly Income

Income	$	4,667
Less Taxes	$ (	702)
Net Spendable Income	$	3,965

Monthly Expenses

Giving	$	400
Housing	$	1,200
Food	$	450
Clothing	$	100
Insurance/Medical	$	300
Automobile/Transportation	$	470
Household/Personal	$	150
Entertainment	$	225
Savings/Investments	$	170
Professional Fees/Services	$	300
Debts	$	200
Total Expenses	$	3,965

Notes:

This mock spending plan assumes expenses for a family of four (two kids) and a wife who works part time. (For illustration purposes only. This is not intended to represent an actual spending plan nor is it to be construed as advice regarding your financial situation.)

We realize that housing prices may be significantly higher on the East and West coasts of the United States

_____

_____

_____

_____

	Net Spendable	-	Total Exp	=	Surplus/(Deficit)
Income vs. Expense	$3,965		$3,965		$0 Surplus

Spending Plan Form and
Spending Plan Sample

SPENDING PLAN SAMPLE
MONTHLY INCOME & EXPENSES

Monthly Income

Income ....$ _____

Less Taxes ....$ (_____)

Net Spendable Income..................$ _____

Monthly Expenses

Giving ....$ _____

Housing ....$ _____

Food ....$ _____

Clothing ....$ _____

Insurance/Medical ....$ _____

Automobile/Transportation ....$ _____

Household/Personal ....$ _____

Entertainment ....$ _____

Savings/Investments......................$ _____

Professional Fees/Services.............$ _____

Debts...$ _____

Total Expenses ....$ _____

Notes:

_____

_____

_____

_____

_____

_____

_____

_____

_____

_____

_____

_____

_____

	Net Spendable	-	Total Exp	=	Surplus/(Deficit)
Income vs. Expense